BARNESBOOK

D1715308

Books by Jackson Mac Low

The Twin Plays: Port-au-Prince & Adams County Illinois
(Mac Low & Bloedow, 1963; 2nd ed. Something Else, 1966)
The Pronouns: A Collection of 40 Dances—for the Dancers
(Mac Low & Judson Dance Workshop, 1964;
2nd ed., Tetrad, 1971; 3rd ed. Station Hill, 1979)
Verdurous Sanguinaria (Southern University, 1967)
August Light Poems (Caterpillar Books, 1967)
22 Light Poems (Black Sparrow, 1968)
23rd Light Poem: For Larry Eigner (Tetrad, 1969)
Stanzas for Iris Lezak (Something Else, 1972)
4 trains (Burning Deck, 1974)
36th Light Poem: In Memoriam Buston Keaton
(Permanent Press, 1975)
21 Matched Asymmetries (Aloes Books, 1978)
54th Light Poem: For Ian Tyson (Membrane, 1978)
A Dozen Douzains for Eve Rosenthal (Gronk Books, 1978)
phone (Printed Editions and Kontexts, 1978)
Asymmetries 1–260 (Printed Editions, 1980)
"Is That Wool Hat My Hat?" (Membrane, 1982)
From Pearl Harbor Day to FDR's Birthday
(Sun & Moon Press, 1982)
French Sonnets (Black Mesa, 1984; 2nd ed., Membrane, 1989)
Bloomsday (Station Hill, 1984)
The Virginia Woolf Poems (Burning Deck, 1985)
Eight Drawing-Asymmetries [boxed serigraphs]
(Francesco Conz, 1985)
Representative Works: 1938–1985 (Roof Books, 1986)
Words nd Ends from Ez (Avenue B, 1989)
Twenties: 100 Poems (Roof Books, 1991)
Pieces O'Six: Thirty Three Poems in Prose (Sun & Moon Press, 1992)
42 Merzgedichte in Memoriam *Kurt Schwitters* (Station Hill, 1994)
Barnesbook (Sun & Moon Press, 1996)

Jackson Mac Low

Barnesbook

Four poems derived from sentences by Djuna Barnes

SUN &
MOON

CLASSICS

127

SUN & MOON PRESS

LOS ANGELES • 1996

Sun & Moon Press
A Program of The Contemporary Arts Educational Project, Inc.
a nonprofit corporation
6026 Wilshire Boulevard, Los Angeles, California 90036

This edition first published in paperback in 1996 by Sun & Moon Press
10 9 8 7 6 5 4 3 2 1
FIRST EDITION
©1996 by Jackson Mac Low
Biographical material ©1996 by Sun & Moon Press
All rights reserved

This book was made possible, in part, through a matching grant from
the National Endowment for the Arts, and through contributions to
The Contemporary Arts Educational Project, Inc.,
a nonprofit corporation

"Barnes 4" was previously published in *O-blēk* magazine.

Cover: Anne Tardos, *From Gentles to Barnesbook*
Design: Katie Messborn
Typography: Guy Bennett

LIBRARY OF CONGRESS CATALOGING IN PUBLICATION DATA
Mac Low, Jackson [1922]
Barnesbook
p. cm — (Sun & Moon Classics: 127)
ISBN: 1-55713-235-6
1. Title. 11. Series.
811'.54—dc20

Printed in the United States of America on acid-free paper.

In Memoriam D. B.

Barnes 1

Once on.

Once like.

Once on the she them sea attention.

That stairs,
"lizard intense?"

Sea she needing man looks?

Mounted brings mounted fifteen.

Pleased looks?

Like asking attention.

Are looks?

Like lizard
Miranda.

"Water"
should.

Crying brings.

Crying asking attention.

Crying:
"Are her vixens you mounted intense?
Know you
with water,
asking stairs:
'Intense?'"

I heard her death,
inordinately heard you.

No journey.

Crying:
"Are call."

Will.

He her;
"fortitude,"
vixen fifteen.

Vixen home.

Miranda.

And attention.

Fifteen.

Miranda.

Fifteen.

Death,
fifteen.

Journey inordinately neither for journey home.

You heard vixen fifteen.

Journey brings are brings mounted brings.

That's to.

They pleased them home.

Love home.

Love looks?

Mounted,
"Love Water"
impersonal asking dead heard death,
that's neither man like
"Are,"
Miranda.

Asking should,
Miranda.

That's what
"sea fortitude,"
stairs,
what
the
"sea fortitude,"
I who man want
"fortitude,"
that you know.

Once
"know."

Know the she them sea.

He
"sea water"
widow's call.

Will wash was was wash us.

Asking:
"How dead what want wash inordinately?"
and
"Who heard
inordinately
inordinately fifteen?"

Inordinately inordinately inordinately inordinately
        inordinately
pleased
pleased she lizard pleased neither mounted
what?

Will with wash.

He her
"fortitude"
said:
"Who are widow's man wash she sea that widow's
        man intense?"

"Vixen water"
and know widow's
"intense"?

Impersonal impersonal attention.

Stairs,
"intense"?

Impersonal impersonal impersonal impersonal
"fortitude,"
nor for that
"fortitude"
attention.

"Fortitude,"
"fortitude,"
"fortitude,"
neither needing said
that death
pleased neither asking:
"Is asking stairs?"
nor crying asking:
"Are for?"

No journey,
Miranda.

Neither needing are dead
"fortitude,"
needing
needing attention.

Stairs,
"intense"?

Vixen journey
"fortitude,"
attention.

Attention.

Attention.

I said:
"Man who brings that needing should a . . ."

Crying them you,
you mounted them.

That's what want you,
you mounted sea,
she who should
should lizard
"know."

Inordinately *who* know?

How looks?

How a widow's like and widow's widow's widow's
        dead heard death,
needing man.

"Are want looks?"

Mounted,
"know."

Looks?

Pleased.

Derived from eight sentences by Djuna Barnes chance-
operationally selected from five of her books and run through
Charles O. Hartman's text-selection program DIASTEXT, a
computer-automation of one of my "diastic" text-selection
procedures first developed in January 1963, and by rule-guided
editing of the program's output. Diastic methods are
nonintentional but do not involve chance operations.

New York: 3–4 August 1989

Barnes 2

Also all;
responsible.

Also the shadows knew such.

The lands away,
responsible shadows,
authors knife-like in them,
knew that they went away then.

"Then were they responsible,
knife-like ledge?"

Weight on locust.

So jug such authors out of such extremity:
each shadow author's responsible and is gentleman's love;
ends have many have cried:
"My reaching,
Meredith,
mercy's shiny or ends us."

As all;
and my floor calendar may dangle an *and*.

He went there.

Then the locust,
caddy to slumber,
those authors she then the calendar creased shiny.

I've speed of building,
estrange the shadows knew farther calendars,
Meredith,
that weight farther slumber and years away,
"Went away reaching,
Sand,"
that the opera's farther floor,
George's innocence,
their eyes my caddy,
can't kill stretching strange calendars,
the abominable calendars,
as having such kills building,
louder calendar is my locust,
my jacket-jumped,
dangle-caddy,
trousers.

I knew plague;
claws that dangle plague;
volume,
then she,
their things in end,
ran seen years,
"Mercy farther reaching,"
innocence building,
her weight having cried such lands.

Then to lift diminishing lift that dangles for down things
and
volume,
Moore below,
locust,
volume,
George and me turned jug,
gentlemen's seen people years,
George,
innocent she,
pair dangle caddy.

"My people stretching have cried reaching,
Meredith,
diminishing my. . ."

To floor
George Moore
and ones
and dangle turned diminishing strange lands
were me were their other tumbler of those knew the ones.

Forgive.

Robin were dangle.

Forgive.

Forgive strange mercy.

He.

My abominable thousand-and-one slumbers.

Forgive my abominable calendar,
abominable,
abominably knife-like
in end—
can't.

Also innocence dangled abandoned innocence'
        unbuttoned bed,
a gentleman's kills.

Also below,
as is.

"I've a reaching— "

"To Robin?—
their diminishing ends' ledge?"

Such the *is* in them.

"Then the ones,
Robin their extremity
of extremity—
with years,
ledge?"

Extremity,
extremity,
extremity,
extremity
were responsible for other and painful ran building,
apart.

To them knew louder locust,
to thousand-and-one creased unbuttoned jugs,
warmer such jacket-jumped,
stile-unbuttoned jacket-jumped,
jacket-jumped,
jacket-jumped,
jacket-jumped,
jacket-jumped,
jacket-jumped
claws' slumber glasses knew lands.

Then to my mug she,
stile things,
the knife-like wall,
the wrong unbuttoned
trousers.

Thousand-and-one abandoned thousand-and-one
        thousand-and-one
thousand-and-one thousand-and-one thousand-and-one
thousand-and-one thousand-and-one things that
knife-like wrong young things that the glasses . . .

"That done,
painful ran ledge?"

Dangle slumber on knife-like wrong,
each kills building,
apart.

Knew
God she floor slumber warmer slumber crease tumbler or ends
"reaching,"
he responsible people's shadows abominably responsible,
knife-like,
responsible responsible responsible for young turned
to the eyes,
kills,
knew weight knife-like turned painful
stretching knife-like abominable claws crease the
strange lands' plague;

I and then she,
louder to their young.

"Then
George *ones* if on opera the stare estrange
God all;
one's locust away,
dangle responsible the turned warmer think ledge?"

Calendar.

Then to the she,
were their shiny crease wrong
George's extremity,
and diminishing with tumbler on their strange
"reaching,"
responsibly diminishing
diminishing diminishing on
in shiny diminishing done
with such seen stretching apart.

Estrange louder out in extremity,
pair locusts,
each other its other
I've estranged their kills and us,
Robin with such locusts'
unbuttoned weight,
unbuttoned unbuttoned innocence,
unbuttoned
eyes the ones on my crease a jug,
tumbler,
mug and she,
their things' shiny beds pair gentlemen's ends.

Who have stretching abominable extremity,
those warmer or such
Dumas-tumbler gentleman's trousers?

Farther ones crease caddy,
or can't end shadows' mercy.

The she floor one's extremity.

The thousand-and-one that . . .

That
I can't;
painful ran the heart the weight.

Then think what their stile in that is,
that is
I've love;
speed down volume,
Sand,
Meredith,
glasses we can't what gentleman's trousers.

Gentlemen's gentlemen stretching gentlemen's
      trousers.

Cried floor volume,
Dumas innocence slumber trousers.

That
Robin jacket-jumped
the stile,
their things' painful painful knife-like love;
I have not cried away
the pair
or said,
that the other operas speed the years,
that
"reaching"
said:
"Sand,"
and away years,
away went lift extremity,
each tumbler o' those that away their two ends.

In
God ones were.

The thousand-and-one have many have cried not.

To estrange strange weight.

Then . . .

"Then mug my pair responsible wrong people dangle slumber
        my
many went away years,
ledge?"

Abandoned heart lands lift.

And George?

Forgive extremity,
in end.

So jug
such authors such abominable claws things speed abandoned
building,
estrange abandoned cases have responsible other kills I lift
a volume,
stile the thousand-and-one things that have seen years,
their hearts' stretching
of *if.*

The bed the tumbler thinks kills building,
"reaching"
innocence' building,
stretching strange mercy cried unbuttoned stretching
        stretching
responsible gentlemen's stretching her weight mercy
        all;
opera glasses stare unbuttoned tumbler done,
speed estrange us not.

Authors:
George's opera estrange,
estrange abandoned us.

As . . .

Derived from five sentences from five books by Djuna Barnes, selected and mixed by chance operations, and fed into Charles O. Hartman's text-selection program DIASTEXT, whose output I edited in accordance with certain rules. DIASTEXT is a computer automation of one of my diastic text-selection methods first developed in January 1963. These methods are *nonintentional* but do not involve chance operations.

New York: 4 August 1989

Barnes 3

Yet I had been here.

"Thou art a niggard!"
the soldiers lament.

"Who brings you tea?"

"Be the whole sleep demands of us,
and light on the heart,
have much."

For a person knew what he was when moved to song—
adding all one's lovers
where no one has had above thrippence worth.

A guilty immunity.

"Render such portions
(or her)
(or them)
(my most favorite)
of the congregation
(the way it is)
live."

"Let *him*."

"Allan or Percy?"

"I know this fine business of nothing ahead of his legs;
that sort of *coup de mort* at first was sad;
and small."

Moydia would supply,
two autumns in spite of the cold,
the good doctor
(or them).

And with his stroke,
his whole recall returned,
his arms swung.

"Should I have any portion of stars in my crown,
as *they* can—
(shall any ?)—
I'll tell you or a man most wondrous."

"*Who* is?"

Yet her favorite art has been immunity
and's been here when her portions lived two autumns.

(The arms crown light legs,
yet are niggard,
bring lovers that are niggard,
who render the whole niggard,
all one's lovers soldiers.)

"Yet *be* niggard,
or thus swung be heart,
be niggard heart,
be thrippence demands."

"One's returned arms demand lament."

"O *them*?"

"Must you demand your tea of *us*?"

Way ahead two whole nothings have immunity.

Should the good lament the cold soldiers' portion,
the soldiers live.

Soldiers' lovers live.

Allan laments legs;
light person he for legs;
guilty her favorite heart,
adding nothing.

"Have they yet tea?"

"Doctor,
supply fine *mort* in the first person,
sort of,
and/or live on."

"Who shall lament live lovers?"

Yet who knew business—
where one's cold and small,
where thrippence a way ahead the soldiers sleep—
was most moved to know man niggard.

One knew when one's lovers adding lovers had swung,
adding favorite portions for whole stars,
no thrippence portions where thrippence sleep returned,
worth no live crown where any man had guilty art
and business returned ahead of autumn's immunity.

"Doctor,
would this crown supply immunity?"

"Percy brings thrippence worth,
the sort his thrippence legs or favorite light person
      moved for worth—
her worth—
above his *first* immunity."

"Doctor,
recall his wondrous portions—
such wondrous portions—
the business of my favorite way,
my most wondrous portion—
was Percy worth such business,
doctor?"

"*Him?*"

"I'll know him with his wondrous stroke—
knew one's favorite man returned cold immunity—
I'll know above them render good men niggard
      lovers."

Ahead was the whole man—
the favorite of the fine congregation.

Nothing was ahead of that congregation.

"Let light have moved lovers stars lament in arms
in any congregation above them—
have any stars' demands moved *him?*"

"Or them?"

"Her fine art recalled Percy's legs,
his niggard person."

"Is Allan adding the crown?"

"All of the fine congregation."

"For thrippence worth of tea?"

"With *him*?"

"Who?"

"Percy."

First this song was sad;
the whole congregation was sad;
nothing let thrippence immunity return.

Percy would recall Moydia.

Moydia'd moved.

The autumn had supplied the *coup de mort*.

The congregation let Percy live.

"Moydia moved Percy,
doctor;
one person had supplied the *coup de mort*,
letting the congregation know the wondrous business."

"What a small *coup*!"

"They know them as much as he swung, man."

"For them this congregation returned demands and rendered
        nothing,
no portions of first light or good cold autumns
or of any small immunity."

"You shall live with his art."

"What shall add most wondrous spite or good small guilt?"

"The whole niggard autumn."

"What whole autumn,
guilty doctor?"

"The one ahead."

"Thou Who shouldst recall most autumns:
let Moydia live the first song:
tell it!"

The first man returned his whole heart,
adding portions of thrippence recall,
soldiers' song or small arms,
sleepy business.

"Doctor,
can you supply my Crown?"

"No."

Here one person brings demands,
Percy's way,
and the doctor brings heart,
his sort.

"I'll tell you most of much."

"Here's Moydia returned,
the favorite song in the heart that stars shall live in;
two persons live in the man:
one's such as renders any worth wondrous;
one renders any portion small."

"Allan would bring them here *two* wondrous portions."

"My portion's most above spite
—or such."

"His two portions have immunity."

"Can they stroke much?"

"His portions have been returned."

"Was art's portion *morte* or way above them?"

"What should strokes add?"

"Much."

"Who knows what art shall add?"

"Much."

"What?"

"When?"

"*They* know."

"Where is the way?"

"Here."

They stroke and sort the *morte* portion,
not knowing when the whole portion'd swung or been for
    them.

"*His* sort knew."

"When?"

Derived from six sentences drawn from five of Djuna Barnes's books by chance-operationally mixing the sentences, repunctuating the mix, inputting the repunctuated mix into Charles O. Hartman's text-selection program DIASTEXT, and finally editing (rearranging, repunctuating, etc.) the program's output. DIASTEXT is Dr. Hartman's first computer-automation of one of my diastic reading-through text-selection methods, first developed in January 1963. These methods are *nonintentional* (since the author cannot predict their results), but do not involve chance operations.

New York: 5–6 August 1989

Barnes 4

Now very never more never more no.

Against around so wondered the whisper against.

Told wondered wandered wondered wandered against.

Wondered her back works.

Wandered back never moved.

She that she mind.

Around she faced—quick.

"Something backs provocation."

Bring things against the ensign the ensign brings up.

Against around so wondered the whisper against.

Wandered back never moved.

Told wondered wandered wondered wandered against.

She that she mind.

Now very never more never more no.

Matter wondered wandered in ensign her very ear.

First whisper.

First whisper whisper whisper in my mysterious was.

Now mysterious Hisodalgus was moving her ear.

Matter wondered wandered in ensign her very ear.

"First in my mysterious mind!"

First.

Something mysterious.

Something.

Something quick.

But whisper quick.

Matter that wondered wandered against the whisper.

Now mysterious Hisodalgus was moving her ear.

More mind.

Wondered her back works.

And ensign moving brings ensign whisper.

Around she faced—quick.

Now to him his Hisodalgus moved.

Matter was very told.

Wondered wandered mysterious.

"Matter wondered wandered mysterious mysterious."

And against the dear ensign moving against the works.

Had her?

Her Medici ways?

Her very matter?

Her Medici back?

Now very never more never more no.

Something of the dear, moving Medici thing?

"Bring around provocation."

Matter that wondered wandered against the whisper.

Now to Greek.

Now to him his Hisodalgus moved.

Now very never more never more no.

Now mysterious Hisodalgus was moving her ear.

And God works.

Around she faced—quick.

Her Medici back?

She that she faced.

"Well, wondered would mind!"

Something Greek around and ground.

Wondered her back works.

Something wall.

Matter against what?

Something of the dear, moving Medici thing?

Moved ensign moving moving in.

Matter was very told.

Hisodalgus to thing the ear.

Her very matter?

Had works.

And to the Greek, ground.

Against around so wondered the whisper against.

She that she faced.

Wandered back never moved.

Wondered her back works.

Now to him his Hisodalgus moved.

Matter wondered wandered in ensign her very ear.

And to the Greek, ground.

Matter no more.

Against around so wondered.

Would her mysterious ways?

Now carry back very dear, carry the more.

She the wall.

Ensign very dear, very dear, carry the ear.

Matter was very told.

Against around so wondered the whisper against.

Would her mysterious ways?

Hisodalgus wondered her told him his mind.

He than the ear and the up.

Had her?

Wondered her back works.

Told mind—faced faced mind!

Something Greek around and ground.

Now would wall.

Something never Greek and Medici ensign.

Her very matter?

Medici provocation around Medici provocation ground.

Hisodalgus wondered her told him his mind.

Around she faced—quick.

The ensign Hisodalgus faced faced provocation well.

And to the Greek, ground.

She that she would mind.

And ensign moving brings ensign whisper.

Wandered back and never moved.

He than the ear and the up.

What?

Wondered her back works.

Now to Greek.

More mind.

Told wondered wandered wondered wandered against.

Her Medici back?

Would her mysterious ways?

Now to him his Hisodalgus moved.

Ensign very dear, very dear, carry the ear.

Matter against what?

She faced provocation.

And against the dear ensign moving against the works.

Wondered wandered mysterious.

He than the ear and the up.

Derived from a chance-operational mix of eight sentences by
Djuna Barnes, selected by chance operations from four of her
books, which was run through Charles O. Hartman's
text-selection program DIASTEXT, an automation of one of
my diastic reading-through text-selection methods developed
in 1963, the output of which was selected and/or rearranged
to form the sentences brought into the quatrains of this poem
by choices often influenced by chance.

New York: 30 August 1989

Afterword

I have been an admirer of the work of Djuna Barnes since the early 1940s when, not long after I had discovered and read her best-known work, the novel *Nightwood*, (and subsequently met in New York Dante Pavone, a nightclub singer who was said to be one of the "layers" of Dr. Matthew Mighty O'Connor), I was introduced to her wonderful archaizing novel *Ryder* by the late Robert Duncan. More recently I discovered her short story collection *Spillway*, her verse play *The Antiphon*, and her early uncollected stories brought together by Douglas Messerli as *Smoke and Other Early Stories*.

Then in June 1989 the poet, scholar, critic, and teacher Charles O. Hartman sent me a computer program called DIASTEXT, which is an automation of one of the "diastic reading-through text-selection methods" that I first developed in January 1963 and have used in various ways since then to compose many poems and performance pieces. These methods are "nonintentional" in that the author cannot predict what will be drawn from a source text, but "deterministic" (as my son, the astrophysicist Mordecai-Mark Mac Low, has pointed out). Most of these methods use a "seed" or "index" word or phrase that is spelled out by reading through a source text to find words that have, successively, the seed's letters in corresponding places, e.g., if I use "Barnes" as the seed and these first two paragraphs as source text, I produce the line:

Barnes early work O'Connor wonderful compose

The seed is used to select words (or other linguistic units) that *spell it through* repeatedly throughout a poem, hence, "diastic" < Gk. *dia* through + *stichos* row, line, verse, on somewhat imperfect analogy with "acrostic": the seed is spelled *through* in the poem's *lines.*

Three books include descriptions of some of my diastic reading-through text-selection methods: *The Pronouns—A Collection of 40 Dances—For the Dancers* (Barrytown, N.Y.: Station Hill, 1979), *The Virginia Woolf Poems* (Providence, R.I.: Burning Deck, 1985), and *Words nd Ends from Ez* (Bolinas, Calif.: Avenue B, 1989), which includes an afterword that describes a "words-nd-ends variant" of one of these methods. Several poems in *Representative Works: 1938–1985* (New York: Roof Books, 1986) were made by diastic methods, notably, the *Pronouns* dances/poems, "The Bluebird Asymmetries," "Let It Go," the "Quatorzains from & for Emily Dickinson," and two section/poems from *Words nd Ends from Ez.* (Some method descriptions have appeared in magazines, e.g., *Temblor* 5 (1987), p. 157.)

One diastic method uses the whole source text as the seed that is spelled out in the poem, e.g., "Let It Go" uses the whole of William Empson's poem of that title as the seed of a poem that spells through *all of his poem* by the words-nd-ends variant method. Hartman's first DIASTEXT program uses the whole source text as seed for a whole-word diastic text selection from itself.

Since 1989 Prof. Hartman has written and sent me five different diastic programs, the last four of which can use seeds other than whole source texts, but the *Barnesbook* poems were made by the method using the whole source text as seed.

I employed DIASTEXT extensively during late June, July, and August 1989, using such sources as sections from Anscombe's English translation of Wittgenstein's *Philosophical Investigations,* Pound's "The Age Demanded an Image" (*Hugh Selwyn Mauberley* II), Landor's "I Strove with None," some of my earlier *42 Merzgedichte in Memoriam Kurt Schwitters* (written 1987–89; Barrytown, NY: Station Hill Press, 1994), and some of my own intuitively written poems from the series *Twenties: 100 Poems* (written 1989–90; New York: Roof Books, 1989).

During this time I sometimes mixed several sources, such as three or more Wittgenstein sections or one of the latter and one "Twenties" poem, often using chance operations to select and combine the sources, and then inputting these mixes into DIASTEXT.

Finally on 5 August I decided to use the five works of Djuna Barnes mentioned above as sources. The actual books used were *The Selected Works of Djuna Barnes* (New York: Farrar, Straus and Cudahy, 1962), comprising *Spillway, The Antiphon,* and *Nightwood; Ryder* (New York: Horace Liveright, 1928); and *Smoke and Other Early Sto-*

ries (College Park, Md.: Sun & Moon Press, 1982). I used chance operations involving irregularly biased random digit triplets to lead me to a chance-determined number of sentences in these works and to mix them. ("Barnes 1" starts from eight of Barnes's sentences, "2" from five of them, "3" from six, and "4" from eight.) I inputted each group of mixed sentences into DIASTEXT and edited the output.

Previously I had only reformatted and repunctuated the raw DIASTEXT output [RDO] and changed some lower-case letters to capitals. Then in July I began deleting many contiguous repetitions of words (though not of sentences, even one-word ones). The whole-word whole-text-as-seed diastic method is especially prone to produce such repetitions, and though they sometimes seem worth keeping (I'm especially fond of the many repetitions of "contradictions" in "Let It Go"), after a time they palled on me. It seemed legitimate to include the option of deleting contiguous word-repetitions in my method, just as I had previously included reformatting, repunctuating, etc.

In writing "Barnes 1–4" I employed these and other editing techniques (e.g., occasionally replacing singulars with plurals), though in "1" and "2" I usually kept contiguous repetitions of lexical words where they fell in the RDO, though I used repeated structure words elsewhere than where they fell. In writing "3," however, I used the RDO mainly as raw material to be extensively rearranged, as well as repunctuated, etc. However, I required myself to use *all the words* of the RDO, including all word-repetitions, and much of the punctuation (leftovers became a picture), usually not far from where they occurred in the RDO. The writing of "Barnes 4" involved even more editing and also discarding. Thus "Barnes 3" and "4" are more copiously edited than the other two poems, and thereby certain narrative and dialogic qualities that had already appeared in "1" and "2" were emphasized and even came to preponderate.

Although my editing tended often to normalize local syntax, I gave DIASTEXT the rein when one of its "abnormally syntactical" lines seemed far superior to anything that my tinkering might effectuate. I freely own that my taste, though strictly guided by certain rules, intervened in the composition of these poems, but some of my compositional methods have long included *rule-guided interaction with nonintentionally-generated materials,* starting with my first poems from chance-given Basic English "nuclei" (May 1961) and including many of my "Light Poems," "The Presidents of the United States of America," *The Pronouns,* etc. (see *Representative Works*).

I've realized over the years that intention and nonintention, "chance" or systematic *nonintentional* determination and "choice," always intricately interact during the composition of even the "purest" or "strictest" chance-operationally or deterministically generated poems. The very devising of methods must involve the author's taste at certain points, even if as many decisions as possible are made by asking questions to be answered by an objectively hazardous oracle or by employing deterministically nonintentional procedures.

The fact that Charles O. Hartman has automated

some of my diastic text-selection methods seems to free me to interact with his programs' outputs in other ways than those required by my "nucleic" methods (as in the poems cited above). But then, this has also always happened in performances of my simultaneities and other indeterminate performance works. Nonintentional operations and intuition seem made for each other! The former free the latter from the pressure of self-expression, that bugaboo decried by Schwitters, for instance, as "injurious to art." Like the seemingly senseless *koan*, the products of nonintentional selective or generative procedures may stimulate intuition to leaps it might never otherwise dare. This has come to seem to me at least as Buddhist as purposefully "nonintentional" methods designed to circumvent the so-called ego. Besides, the obscurely manifold resources of the individual mind, when called upon directly as well as obliquely, produce a "richer" poetry, and a poet writes primarily to help the poems come to be, though making artworks for their own sake *is* a way of *pursuing* one's salvation with diligence.

While finally revising this afterword in February 1995, I have begun to wonder what Ms. Barnes would have thought of my making poems in these weird ways from her sentences. Would she have been indignant, considered my borrowings and rearrangements of her words desecrations of her texts? Or would she have accepted these poems as acts of homage? It is strange to carry on such a "dialogue" with a person who is present only in her writings and in a steadily decreasing number of living memories. It is only a dialogue by courtesy, since Djuna Barnes cannot speak back except through her texts. I hope she would have come to enjoy these poems and to realize the spirit in which they were written.

Jackson Mac Low
New York
29 August 1989
18 October 1994
7 – 9 February 1995

JACKSON MAC LOW

Poet, composer, essayist, performance artist, playwright, and painter, Jackson Mac Low was born in Chicago on September 12, 1922. His poetry began to be published in 1941. Since 1954 he has often employed chance operations and other nonintentional procedures, as well as intentional techniques, when composing verbal, musical, theatrical, and multimedia performance works. Mac Low's turn to nonintentional methods was inspired by Zen Buddhism (as taught by Dr. D.T. Suzuki), the *I Ching* ("Book of Changes"), and John Cage and his music composed in the early 1950s by chance operations, some of which is indeterminate of its performance (as are many of Mac Low's works).

By the middle 1960s, Mac Low was well known for his readings, performances, and theater works. *The Marrying Maiden*, a play chance-operationally derived (1958–59) from the *I Ching*, was performed by The Living Theatre in New York (1960–61), directed by Judith Malina, with decor by Julian Beck and music by Mr. Cage. His *Verdurous Sanguinaria* (written 1961; published 1967), was premiered in 1961 during his first concert, produced by the composer La Monte Young, in Yoko Ono's New York loft. His *Twin Plays* (written and premiered in 1963) constitute his first book (1963, 1966). Selections from *The Pronouns*, forty poems that are instructions for dancers (written 1964; published 1964, 1971, 1979), were first performed in 1965 by Meredith Monk and a group organized by her.

In 1963, with its editor Mr. Young, Mac Low co-published the first edition of *An Anthology*, which through George Maciunas (who designed it in 1961) gave rise to Fluxus, of which Mac Low was the first literary editor and whose festivals gave him his first European performances (1962–63). Subsequently, many works written in and after 1960 were published, notably *August Light Poems* (1967), *22 Light Poems* (1968), *Stanzas for Iris Lezak* (1972), *4 trains* (1974), *21 Matched Asymmetries* (1978), *A Dozen Douzains for Eve Rosenthal* (1978), *phone* (1978), *Asymmetries 1–260* (1980), and *"Is That Wool Hat My Hat?"* (1982).

On his sixtieth birthday, in 1982, poets, composers, instrumentalists, dancers, and performance artists joined in an eight-hour retrospective of his work at Washington Square Church in New York. Clearly an influence on the decade, Mac Low, in *From Pearl Harbor Day to FDR's Birthday* (Sun & Moon, 1982) and *Bloomsday* (1984) evinced his reawakened interest in intentionally disjunctive writing (which he had practiced intermittently since the 1930s) aroused partly by his reading of so-called Language writers. Since 1980 he has employed both intentional and nonintentional methods in his writing, music, visual art, and multimedia performance and radio works (produced and broadcast mainly by Westdeutscher Rundfunk, Cologne), both usually realized with his wife, Anne Tardos.

Representative Works: 1938–1985 (1986) is a "sampler" showing the wide range of Mac Low's contributions in many fields. Other recent books include *French Sonnets* (1984, 1989), *The Virginia Woolf Poems* (1985), *Words nd Ends from Ez* (1989), and *Twenties* (1991). His *42 Merzgedichte* in Memoriam *Kurt Schwitters* won the America Award for the best new work of poetry in 1994.

SUN & MOON CLASSICS

PIERRE ALFERI [France]
Natural Gaits 95 (1-55713-231-3, $10.95)
The Familiar Path of the Fighting Fish [in preparation]

CLAES ANDERSSON [Finland]
What Became Words 121 (1-55713-231-3, $11.95)

DAVID ANTIN [USA]
Death in Venice: Three Novellas [in preparation]
Selected Poems: 1963–1973 10 (1-55713-058-2, $13.95)

ECE AYHAN [Turkey]
A Blind Cat AND *Orthodoxies* [in preparation]

DJUNA BARNES [USA]
Ann Portuguise [in preparation]
The Antiphon [in preparation]
At the Roots of the Stars: The Short Plays 53 (1-55713-160-0, $12.95)
Biography of Julie von Bartmann [in preparation]
The Book of Repulsive Women 59 (1-55713-173-2, $6.95)
Collected Stories 110 (1-55713-226-7, $24.95 [cloth])
Interviews 86 (0-940650-37-1, $12.95)
New York 5 (0-940650-99-1, $12.95)
Smoke and Other Early Stories 2 (1-55713-014-0, $9.95)

CHARLES BERNSTEIN [USA]
Content's Dream: Essays 1975–1984 49 (0-940650-56-8, $14.95)
Dark City 48 (1-55713-162-7, $11.95)
Republics of Reality: 1975–1995 [in preparation]
Rough Trades 14 (1-55713-080-9, $10.95)

JENS BJØRNEBOE [Norway]
The Bird Lovers 43 (1-55713-146-5, $9.95)
Semmelweis [in preparation]

ANDRÉ DU BOUCHET [France]
The Indwelling [in preparation]
Today the Day [in preparation]
Where Heat Looms 87 (1-55713-238-0, $12.95)

ANDRÉ BRETON [France]
Arcanum 17 51 (1-55713-170-8, $12.95)
Earthlight 26 (1-55713-095-7, $12.95)

DAVID BROMIGE [b. England/Canada]
  The Harbormaster of Hong Kong 32 (1-55713-027-2, $10.95)
  My Poetry [in preparation]

MARY BUTTS [England]
  Scenes from the Life of Cleopatra 72 (1-55713-140-6, $13.95)

OLIVIER CADIOT [France]
  Art Poétique [in preparation]

PAUL CELAN [b. Bukovina/France]
  Breathturn 74 (1-55713-218-6, $12.95)

LOUIS-FERDINAND CÉLINE [France]
  Dances without Music, without Dancers, without Anything
    [in preparation]

CLARK COOLIDGE [USA]
  The Crystal Text 99 (1-55713-230-5, $11.95)
  Own Face 39 (1-55713-120-1, $10.95)
  The Rova Improvisations 34 (1-55713-149-X, $11.95)
  Solution Passage: Poems 1978–1981 [in preparation]
  This Time We Are One/City in Regard [in preparation]

ROSITA COPIOLI [Italy]
  The Blazing Lights of the Sun 84 (1-55713-195-3, $11.95)

RENÉ CREVEL [France]
  Are You Crazy? [in preparation]
  Babylon 65 (1-55713-196-1, $12.95)
  Difficult Death [in preparation]

MILO DE ANGELIS [Italy]
  Finite Intuition: Selected Poetry and Prose 65 (1-55713-068-X, $11.95)

HENRI DELUY [France]
  Carnal Love 121 (1-55713-272-0, $11.95)

RAY DIPALMA [USA]
  The Advance on Messmer [in preparation]
  Numbers and Tempers: Selected Early Poems 24
    (1-55713-099-X, $11.95)

HEIMITO VON DODERER [Austria]
  The Demons 13 (1-55713-030-2, $29.95)
  Every Man a Murderer 66 (1-55713-183-X, $14.95)
  The Merowingians [in preparation]

JOSÉ DONOSO [Chile]
Hell Has No Limits 101 (1-55713-187-2, $10.95)

ARKADII DRAGOMOSCHENKO [Russia]
Description 9 (1-55713-075-2, $11.95)
Phosphor [in preparation]
Xenia 29 (1-55713-107-4, $12.95)

JOSÉ MARIA DE EÇA DE QUEIROZ [Portugal]
The City and the Mountains [in preparation]
The Mandarins [in preparation]

LARRY EIGNER [USA]
readiness / enough / depends / on [in preparation]

RAYMOND FEDERMAN [b. France/USA]
Smiles on Washington Square 60 (1-55713-181-3, $10.95)
The Twofold Vibration [in preparation]

RONALD FIRBANK [England]
Santal 58 (1-55713-174-0, $7.95)

DOMINIQUE FOURCADE [France]
Click-Rose 94 (1-55713-264-X, $10.95)
Xbo 35 (1-55713-067-1, $9.95)

SIGMUND FREUD [Austria]
Delusion and Dream in Wilhelm Jensen's GRADIVA 38
(1-55713-139-2, $11.95)

MAURICE GILLIAMS [Belgium/Flanders]
Elias, or The Struggle with the Nightingales 79 (1-55713-206-2, $12.95)

LILIANE GIRAUDON [France]
Fur 114 (1-55713-222-4, $12.95)
Pallaksch, Pallaksch 61 (1-55713-191-0, $12.95)

ALFREDO GIULIANI [Italy]
Ed. *I Novissimi: Poetry for the Sixties* 55
(1-55713-137-6, $14.95)
Verse and Nonverse [in preparation]

TED GREENWALD [USA]
Going into School that Day [in preparation]
Licorice Chronicles [in preparation]

BARBARA GUEST [USA]
  Defensive Rapture 30 (1-55713-032-9, $11.95)
  Fair Realism 41 (1-55713-245-3, $10.95)
  Moscow Mansions [in preparation]
  Seeking Air [in preparation]
  Selected Poems [in preparation]

HERVÉ GUIBERT [France]
  Ghost Image 93 (1-55713-276-4, $13.95)

KNUT HAMSUN [Norway]
  Rosa [in preparation]
  Under the Autumn Star [in preparation]
  Victoria 69 (1-55713-177-5, $10.95)
  Wayfarers 88 (1-55713-211-9, $13.95)
  The Wanderer Plays on Muted Strings [in preparation]
  The Women at the Pump 115 (1-55713-244-5, $14.95)

MARTIN A. HANSEN [Denmark]
  The Liar 111 (1-55713-243-7, $12.95)

THOMAS HARDY [England]
  Jude the Obscure 77 (1-55713-203-8, $12.95)

PAAL-HELGE HAUGEN [Norway]
  Wintering with the Light 107 (1-55713-273-9, $10.95)

MARIANNE HAUSER [b. Alsace-Lorraine/USA]
  The Long and the Short: Selected Stories [in preparation]
  Me & My Mom 36 (1-55713-175-9, $9.95)
  Prince Ishmael 4 (1-55713-039-6, $11.95)

JOHN HAWKES [USA]
  The Owl AND *The Goose on the Grave* 67 (1-55713-194-5, $12.95)

LYN HEJINIAN [USA]
  The Cell 21 (1-55713-021-3, $11.95)
  The Cold of Poetry 42 (1-55713-063-9, $12.95)
  My Life 11 (1-55713-024-8, $9.95)
  Writing Is an Aid to Memory 141 (1-55713-271-2, $9.95)

EMMANUEL HOCQUARD [France]
  The Cape of Good Hope [in preparation]

SIGURD HOEL [Norway]
  The Road to the World's End 75 (1-55713-210-0, $13.95)

FANNY HOWE [USA]
  The Deep North 15 (1-55713-105-8, $9.95)
  Radical Love: A Trilogy [in preparation]
  Saving History 27 (1-55713-100-7, $12.95)

SUSAN HOWE [USA]
  The Europe of Trusts 7 (1-55713-009-4, $10.95)

LAURA (RIDING) JACKSON [USA]
  Lives of Wives 71 (1-55713-182-1, $12.95)

HENRY JAMES [USA]
  The Awkward Age [in preparation]
  What Maisie Knew [in preparation]

LEN JENKIN [USA]
  Dark Ride and Other Plays 22 (1-55713-073-6, $13.95)
  Careless Love 54 (1-55713-168-6, $9.95)
  Pilgrims of the Night: Five Plays [in preparation]

WILHELM JENSEN [Germany]
  Gradiva 38 (1-55713-139-2, $13.95)

JEFFREY M. JONES [USA]
  The Crazy Plays and Others [in preparation]
  J. P. Morgan Saves the Nation 157 (1-55713-256-9, $9.95)
  Love Trouble 78 (1-55713-198-8, $9.95)
  Night Coil [in preparation]

STEVE KATZ [USA]
  Florry of Washington Heights [in preparation]
  43 Fictions 18 (1-55713-069-8, $12.95)
  Swanny's Ways [in preparation]
  Wier & Pouce [in preparation]

ALEXEI KRUCHENYKH [Russia]
  Suicide Circus: Selected Poems [in preparation]

THOMAS LA FARGE [USA]
  Terror of Earth 136 (1-55713-261-5, $11.95)

VALERY LARBAUD [France]
  Childish Things 19 (1-55713-119-8, $13.95)

OSMAN LINS [Brazil]
  Nine, Novena 104 (1-55713-229-1, $12.95)

NATHANIEL MACKEY [USA]
  Bedouin Hornbook [in preparation]

JACKSON MAC LOW [USA]
  Barnesbook 127 (1-55713-235-6, $9.95)
  From Pearl Harbor Day to FDR's Birthday 126
    (0-940650-19-3, $10.95)
  Pieces O' Six 17 (1-55713-060-4, $11.95)
  Two Plays [in preparation]

CLARENCE MAJOR [USA]
  Painted Turtle: Woman with Guitar (1-55713-085-x, $11.95)

F. T. MARINETTI [Italy]
  Let's Murder the Moonshine: Selected Writings 12
    (1-55713-101-5, $13.95)
  The Untameables 28 (1-55713-044-7, $10.95)

HARRY MATHEWS [USA]
  Selected Declarations of Dependence (1-55713-234-8, $10.95)

FRIEDRIKE MAYRÖCKER [Austria]
  with each clouded peak [in preparation]

DOUGLAS MESSERLI [USA]
  After [in preparation]
  Ed. *50: A Celebration of Sun & Moon Classics* 50
  (1-55713-132-5, $13.95)
  Ed. *From the Other Side of the Century: A New American
    Poetry 1960–1990* 47 (1-55713-131-7, $29.95)
  Ed. [with Mac Wellman] *From the Other Side of the
    Century II: A New American Drama 1960–1995* [in preparation]
  River to Rivet: A Poetic Trilogy [in preparation]

DAVID MILLER [England]
  The River of Marah [in preparation]

CHRISTOPHER MORLEY [USA]
  Thunder on the Left 68 (1-55713-190-2, $12.95)

GÉRARD DE NERVAL [France]
  Aurelia [in preparation]

VALÈRE NOVARINA [France]
  The Theater of the Ears 85 (1-55713-251-8, $13.95)

CHARLES NORTH [USA]
  New and Selected Poems [in preparation]

TOBY OLSON [USA]
  Dorit in Lesbos [in preparation]
  Utah [in preparation]

MAGGIE O'SULLIVAN [England]
  Palace of Reptiles [in preparation]

SERGEI PARADJANOV [Armenia]
  Seven Visions [in preparation]

ANTONIO PORTA [Italy]
  Metropolis [in preparation]

ANTHONY POWELL [England]
  Afternoon Men [in preparation]
  Agents and Patients [in preparation]
  From a View to a Death [in preparation]
  O, How the Wheel Becomes It! 76 (1-55713-221-6, $10.95)
  Venusburg [in preparation]
  What's Become of Waring [in preparation]

SEXTUS PROPERTIUS [Ancient Rome]
  Charm 89 (1-55713-224-0, $11.95)

RAYMOND QUENEAU [France]
  Children of Clay [in preparation]

CARL RAKOSI [USA]
  Poems 1923–1941 64 (1-55713-185-6, $12.95)

TOM RAWORTH [England]
  Eternal Sections 23 (1-55713-129-5, $9.95)

NORBERTO LUIS ROMERO [Spain]
  The Arrival of Autumn in Constantinople [in preparation]

AMELIA ROSSELLI [Italy]
  War Variations [in preparation]

JEROME ROTHENBERG [USA]
  Gematria 45 (1-55713-097-3, $11.95)

SEVERO SARDUY [Cuba]
  From Cuba with a Song 52 (1-55713-158-9, $10.95)

ALBERTO SAVINIO [Italy]
  Selected Stories [in preparation]

LESLIE SCALAPINO [USA]
  Defoe 46 (1-55713-163-5, $14.95)

ARTHUR SCHNITZLER [Austria]
Dream Story 6 (1-55713-081-7, $11.95)
Lieutenant Gustl 37 (1-55713-176-7, $9.95)

GILBERT SORRENTINO [USA]
The Orangery 91 (1-55713-225-9, $10.95)

ADRIANO SPATOLA [Italy]
Collected Poetry [in preparation]

GERTRUDE STEIN [USA]
How to Write 83 (1-55713-204-6, $12.95)
Mrs. Reynolds 1 (1-55713-016-7, $13.95)
Stanzas in Meditation 44 (1-55713-169-4, $11.95)
Tender Buttons 8 (1-55713-093-0, $9.95)
To Do [in preparation]
Winning His Way and Other Poems [in preparation]

GIUSEPPE STEINER [Italy]
Drawn States of Mind 63 (1-55713-171-6, $8.95)

ROBERT STEINER [USA]
Bathers [in preparation]
The Catastrophe 134 (1-55713-232-1, $26.95 [cloth])

JOHN STEPPLING [USA]
Sea of Cortez and Other Plays 96 (1-55713-237-2, $14.95)

STIJN STREUVELS [Belgium/Flanders]
The Flaxfield 3 (1-55713-050-7, $11.95)

ITALO SVEVO [Italy]
As a Man Grows Older 25 (1-55713-128-7, $12.95)

JOHN TAGGART [USA]
Crosses [in preparation]
Loop 150 (1-55713-012-4, $11.95)

FIONA TEMPLETON [Scotland]
Delirium of Interpretations [in preparation]

SUSANA THÉNON [Argentina]
distancias / distances 40 (1-55713-153-8, $10.95)

JALAL TOUFIC [Lebanon]
Over-Sensitivity 119 (1-55713-270-4, $13.95)

TCHICAYA U TAM'SI [The Congo]
The Belly [in preparation]

PAUL VAN OSTAIJEN [Belgium/Flanders]
The First Book of Schmoll [in preparation]

CARL VAN VECHTEN [USA]
Parties 31 (1-55713-029-9, $13.95)
Peter Whiffle [in preparation]

TARJEI VESAAS [Norway]
The Great Cycle [in preparation]
The Ice Palace 16 (1-55713-094-9, $11.95)

KEITH WALDROP [USA]
The House Seen from Nowhere [in preparation]
Light While There Is Light: An American History 33
  (1-55713-136-8, $13.95)

WENDY WALKER [USA]
The Sea-Rabbit or, The Artist of Life 57 (1-55713-001-9, $12.95)
The Secret Service 20 (1-55713-084-1, $13.95)
Stories Out of Omarie 58 (1-55713-172-4, $12.95)

BARRETT WATTEN [USA]
Frame (1971–1991) [in preparation]

MAC WELLMAN [USA]
The Land Beyond the Forest: Dracula AND *Swoop* 112
  (1-55713-228-3, $12.95)
The Land of Fog and Whistles: Selected Plays [in preparation]
Two Plays: A Murder of Crows AND *The Hyacinth Macaw* 62
  (1-55713-197-X, $11.95)

JOHN WIENERS [USA]
707 Scott Street 106 (1-55713-252-6, $12.95)

ÉMILE ZOLA [France]
The Belly of Paris 70 (1-55713-066-3, $14.95)

*

Individuals order from:
Sun & Moon Press
6026 Wilshire Boulevard
Los Angeles, California 90036
213-857-1115

Libraries and Bookstores in the United States and Canada
should order from:
Consortium Book Sales & Distribution
1045 Westgate Drive, Suite 90
Saint Paul, Minnesota 55114-1065
800-283-3572
FAX 612-221-0124

Libraries and Bookstores in the United Kingdom and on the Continent
should order from:
Password Books Ltd.
23 New Mount Street
Manchester M4 4DE, ENGLAND
0161 953 4009
INTERNATIONAL +44 61 953-4009
0161 953 4090